100 TIME HACKS
FOR THE INSANELY BUSY WOMAN

BY
DR. TONYA LYNN HENDERSON

PREFACE:

---

100 Time Hacks for the Insanely Busy Woman is a gift to the modern woman. If you, like so many others, wear three hats at once and you know the value of recapturing a few minutes here and there, then this book is for you. I, like so many members of Generation-X, have been there and back, juggling career, family, and creative work along the way. My experiences as a military officer, a working mother, nontraditional student, Cub Scout leader, chemo-buddy, teacher, and entrepreneur have offered numerous opportunities to get really good at juggling—really, really good at juggling! Many of these lessons were learned the hard way, including some that amount to nothing more than common sense. It's embarrassing to admit it, but I know that when we are insanely busy, we don't always notice the simple, subtle ways that we might gain a little efficiency here and there.

What if you could find simple ways to squeeze more and more life into every minute of every day? If you need more time to parent, more time to work, more time to learn, more time to have fun, more time to follow your dreams . . . this book is for you! The purpose of this book is to share ideas about squeezing more life into our days without driving ourselves and everyone else crazy in the process. In full disclosure, I must admit that I haven't always been very successful with the second half of that last suggestion, but I am constantly improving and hope that reading this little book will help you in that regard.

In this book you will learn how to:

- Squeeze more life into your busy day

- Make the most of your time at home and at work

- Find a little "me time" without neglecting your many responsibilities

- Avoid time-consuming problems by investing mere seconds to prevent them

- Identify repeating problems that will continue to cost you precious time if not addressed

- Get focused and stay that way to maximize your productivity over the long haul

Are you ready to begin? Why not take the quiz at the end of the book to see where you fit in the spectrum? Are you *insanely busy*, or *happily busy* and managing just fine? Most of us fall somewhere in between the extremes, but I have yet to meet a truly productive or accomplished person who wouldn't like a few more minutes here and there to get things done or just breathe!

I hope you enjoy the journey, and even have a laugh or two, on your way to getting more done in less time.

Best wishes— Tonya

ABOUT THE AUTHOR

Photograph by Tenacious Photography

http://www.tenaciousphoto.com/

Dr. Tonya L. Henderson

Purveyor of Organizational Clarity

Leader | Learner | Storyteller

tlhenderson@tonya.today   www.tonya.today

Dr. Tonya L. Henderson is an expert in organization development and change. She lives in Colorado Springs, Colorado, where she works as a freelance researcher and consultant. As a Doctor of Management and a graduate of the US Naval Academy, she blends original research with a military officer's practicality. A veteran of the aerospace industry, her work is informed by multi-disciplinary experience, education, and scholarship.

Tonya loves exploring the ways in which groups of people self-organize and how repeated patterns of perceptions, communications, and behaviors offer clues to organizational values and outcomes. An experienced keynote speaker, Dr. Henderson has been featured at TEDxColoradoSprings and the Story Project. She enjoys teaching business research, management, and strategy, and currently serves as the Professional Development Workshop Chairman for the Academy of Management's Management Consulting Division. Dr. Henderson has co-authored two academic books, numerous book chapters, papers, and articles and always has multiple projects in work for both academic and business audiences. Currently serving as the Curator for TEDxColoradoSprings, she has thoroughly enjoyed working with a team of talented volunteers to create this year's event, themed *To Be of Service*.

Links to her blog, publications, and business endeavors can be found at www.tonya.today.

TABLE OF CONTENTS

INTRODUCTION

Do you feel guilty if you sit down to watch a TV show or—luxury of all luxuries—eat your dinner before it gets cold?

Are you always "on duty," beholden to someone or something even into the wee hours of the night? Every night? Does taking the time to blow-dry your hair seem like a distant dream from your carefree youth? Did you give up on manicures because sitting still for an hour seems impossible? Do you have time for a doctor's appointment but no time to exercise? Are you so busy DOING things that BEING who you are is something that seldom crosses your mind, except of course when the overwhelm sets in?

If you answered "yes" to any of the above questions, you might very well be an insanely busy woman, what I affectionately call an IBW.

Before you begin, let's get something straight. I don't want you to read this book from cover to cover if that doesn't seem fun and useful to you. This book is not another "should" on your to-do list. Please DO NOT add a line with a checkmark that says, "Read a time management book!" After all, *who has time for that?* Instead, I would ask you to commit to one simple thing—pick a section that addresses your most stressing pain point and try one or two items from that section. Do not feel compelled to take them in order or to try every item in that section. Our journeys are all different, and if you try to follow a recipe designed for someone else, failure is quite likely. Just choose the things that appeal to you personally and give them a shot. If they don't work after a few days, move on and try something new, whether it comes from this book or another source.

What matters here is YOU. YOUR experience. YOUR frustrations. YOUR coping, general happiness and—dare I say it?—

your SAFETY. Yes. *Safety*. How many car wrecks happen because we are running late, overtaxed, and not paying attention?

I am reminded of a sunny fall day just two years ago when I was heading up to the mountains to do a little writing. I was sitting at a red light, waiting for it to change, when I noticed the grill of a large sport utility vehicle getting closer and closer in the rearview mirror of my Prius. Just as I thought, "She's not going to stop," she hit me. Luckily, no one was injured, and her insurance covered the damage to my bumper, but things could have been much worse. The woman in the other car had two young teens with her and was late taking them to a soccer practice. In a hurry, and frantic to say the least, she had been too preoccupied to notice the red light or the little red car blocking her path.

Thankfully, it turned out to be nothing more than an inconvenience for all concerned, but I have to wonder. If the other driver had been able to shave off a few minutes from her busy day here and there, buying her a little extra time to get kids, cleats, snacks, and keys into the car and on the road, could the wreck have been avoided? Maybe . . . .

That day, as she waited for her husband to arrive and the police took down our information, I remember thinking, "That used to be me." How could I be angry when it was just dumb luck that had kept me from doing the same thing a few short years earlier?

I silently recalled the days when I had been in her shoes, perpetually late to get my kids to a club or practice, flying into the parking lot on a wing and a prayer. Since we didn't even have GPS in the car or on our phones back then, there was usually a considerable amount of time spent looking for the place where we were supposed to be as well. My oldest son, panic in his eyes, would jump out of the car the second it stopped to rush in the door, perpetually embarrassed to be the last one there for his activities. Guilty as charged. I was NOT the poster child for on-time arrivals for quite some time, although I worked at it and got better and better over time. The tips and tricks I will share with you in this book were developed over time, as I solved that problem and several others that popped up along the way to where I am today.

Where am I now? I am a person who gets a lot done rather quickly, but capitalizes on the perpetual room for improvement that we all have to work with both personally and professionally.

How did I come to write this book? It's a long story. I have been a daughter, wife, mother, aerospace worker, military officer, student, yoga instructor, professor, writer, speaker, leader of a nonprofit, and a volunteer. For some strange reason, I typically feel compelled to wear several of these hats at once. (Does this sound familiar?)

At first, I thought the state of overwhelm was tied to a lack of focus. So I worked hard to figure out what I wanted and how to get it. Then, once I zoomed in on my life's purpose (organizational clarity), I still found that the work I WANTED to do far exceeded the number of waking hours available to do it! Even after I learned the magic of aligning my personal and professional resources and time with that mission, mastered (or so I thought) the art of gracefully saying "no" when overtaxed, and declared victory over my own indecision, I STILL found myself feeling overextended at times. It's insidious. Being too busy sneaks up on you, like a mischievous sibling hoping to make you jump out of your chair. We get into the habit of rushing around *doing things*, becoming less and less attuned to our surroundings. Then the universe starts to send us little warning signs, and if we are too busy to pick up on them, the lessons get harder and harder to bear, with bigger and bigger consequences until we learn to change our behavior.

I will share two fairly recent personal examples. The first happened a few years ago. The second was more subtle, but it's so fresh in my mind that I am still telling the story to friends and enjoying a laugh with the lesson.

Story #1: Road Warrior Princess vs. Bambi

A few years ago, I was trying to rebuild my life after a series of stressful events, and I took a part-time job teaching night school about 60 miles from my home. It was a great opportunity for me. The classes were fun, and the students were cool. I loved it. They came from all over the world and were both eager to learn and genuinely interested. (Cue harp music.) There was one small problem. The job involved a lengthy commute—at night, occasionally in a snowstorm, on a road that seemed to be a favorite hang-out of all of the deer in Southern Colorado. No kidding. The stretch of highway between me and my beloved classroom was the deer equivalent of a crowded singles bar during two-for-one happy hour.

One night, as I drove to class, I glanced down to change the radio station in my little red Prius that I dearly love. I don't think I took my eyes off of the road for more than a second or two, but when I looked up, my windshield was filled with . . . well . . . deer butt! I was looking squarely at the back side of a large buck that was bouncing across the road in front of me. Instinctively I braked and swerved, staying on the road (whew!) and miraculously not hitting him straight on. I heard a nerve-wracking scraping sound come from the right front fender. I straightened myself on the road and kept driving, looking for a safe place to pull over. That took a few minutes, and as I drove on, I realized that the car and I both still seemed to be intact, although poor Bambi and the fender must have both suffered some damage. I was sure that at least a hoof had hit the car, and hard! When I finally found a lighted parking lot, I pulled in and fearfully got out of the car to inspect the damage. I walked around the front end, wincing as I thought of what my right front fender must look like, and found that there was not a single scratch on the car. Nothing! Not even a tiny little mark! There was no evidence whatsoever of my brush with death or deer! Apparently, my hoofed companion had gotten out of the way in time. As the grim reaper shook his head and vowed to try and get Bambi and me both another day, I decided to quit that job and look for something closer to home.

In the more recent past, I realized that having four (Yes, four!) jobs at one time was not sustainable for me. Who'd have guessed? I was getting a bit frazzled. Teaching yoga, although it was something I enjoyed, was time-consuming and was not paying the bills, so I decided to take a yoga sabbatical. I talked with the studio owner where I had been a regular instructor for about two and a half years and agreed to a date when a new teacher could take over my weekly classes. That was really hard for me, especially since jobs at that studio are in demand. I knew that if I gave up my spot, there was no guarantee that I could return later on. Yet when I looked at the hours available to me, the time spent commuting to practice where I teach, and the fact that I needed to make more time to practice myself, there was only one choice that was sustainable for me. My problem was solved, and I felt a huge sense of relief. The following week, I gave my students one of the best yoga classes that I have ever taught. The people who came were wonderful, and I felt connected to them as I guided them through the postures, tailoring the teaching to maximize their benefit. I even gave a nice little spiel on mindfulness that was well received. (A happy teacher moment!) I said my goodbyes, cleaned up the practice room, and then it hit me—just before I closed up the studio to leave—my yoga pants were on backwards! Clearly, the time had come for me to take a break!

Okay, lady! Enough goofy stories about listening to the universe! After all, I, the reader, am in a hurry! I bought this book because I

AM an insanely busy woman! Why are you taking up my time with fender benders, Bambi, and yoga pants?

The answer is simple. When we are *insanely busy*, these kinds of things are more prone to happen. Managing time better isn't just about feeding the achievement monster or trying to be a super-mom and CEO at the same time. It's about getting our collective act together so that the people who love us are not stressed out by our very presence. It's about getting focused and centered enough to accomplish what we dream of. It's about picking a direction and *moving* in it.

I first wrote a short version of this book in 2015 for a female entrepreneurs' networking group I was a member of at the time, radio host Janiece Carlson's *Step up to Success of Colorado Springs*. I gave them a little talk on time management for entrepreneurs and provided the mini-book, *50 Ways to Make Friends With Father Time*, as a gift. Building on the original 50 tips in that book, I have collected and test-driven many more, culled out some of the less helpful ones, and arranged them to help you find what you need for your unique situation.

Okay. That's enough talking about it.

Let's DO it! Without further ado, I give you a *100 Time Hacks for the Insanely Busy Woman.*

QUICK FIXES FOR EVERYONE

How many jobs do you have? How many roles do you fill at once? How many people count on you to do important work, take care of them, or create a happy home? We all seem to wear a LOT of hats—something, I have come to realize, is not all that uncommon among today's insanely busy women (IBWs). After all, if we only had one job and only ourselves to think of, most of us would alternate between boredom and loneliness. Today's women play a much bigger game, one that seems to be expanding as we become more aware of the need for self-care in the midst of career accomplishment and family obligations.

I have left a lot of blood on the battlefield, figuratively of course, where this little book is concerned. As the list of life experiences in the introduction suggests, I am not as young as I once was, and yet I find myself in the throes of building my third career and as busy as ever. My kids are grown, and yet I am perpetually *doing things*, with different responsibilities and tasks but the same level of activity across the board.

The lessons in this section are intended to be of use to all women, regardless of your season of life. Whether you are young or old, a PTA president, or a CEO of a Fortune 500, an empty-nester like me or happily raising a house full of children, this section is for you! Some items are rather simple, obvious things that may cause you to roll your eyes if you already do them. Others may strike you as new or even—I hope—innovative. Either way, I invite you to test drive them and see what works for your unique situation.

Ask, and you shall receive! This is the hardest advice for me to follow myself. However, it is important enough to be the first item in this book. I am constantly amazed at how easy it is to get help once I convince myself to ask. As a business owner, teacher, and executive director of a small nonprofit, there are so many things to think about that executing it all myself would be utterly impossible. I have to either ask for help regularly and assertively and follow-up, or make a choice to play a smaller game both personally and professionally. One of these days, I will get used to it, but I remain thrilled and delighted almost every day when people help me get things done. When it's a matter of people doing their jobs, they delight me with high quality. When it's a favor, the grace and generosity of my friends and colleagues never fail to shine through. Yet, a few short years ago, I had a very different perspective, one that required a mental shift on my part, one that allowed me to step back into leadership roles after a long hiatus. Somewhere along the way, I had become afraid of failing and, for a while, didn't outsource much of anything. That was one of the problems with what I now affectionately refer to as "my starter business," a business that I closed after years of struggling to make it work.

Headset magic. Wearing headphones or even earbuds while working (at home or in an office cubicle) serves two purposes. First, it can be nice, and helpful, to play some instrumental music in the background while working, provided you work in a setting where doing so doesn't create a safety hazard. (If you operate heavy equipment or perform delicate surgery, this might not be so wise.) It drowns out background noise, improves your mood, and helps you stay upbeat (or relaxed, depending on what you need). Second, it sends a clear message to those who would otherwise be tempted to interrupt your focus. For example, if I have a lot of work to get done on an airplane, wearing headphones can allow me to remain in my work bubble without being rude to a seatmate who might otherwise engage me in conversation. I am sure the guy in the next seat is a cool person, but I need to finish my report right now! I'll socialize after I save the file and stow my laptop for landing.

Consider making yourself more efficient at home, not just at work. Think in terms of life–work integration. You are one person, even if you wear many hats. Saving an hour at home by putting something in the crockpot before you leave for the office can easily translate into an extra hour of sleep, or maybe even time to review your notes for tomorrow's meeting.

Work it out. My favorite yoga studio is 30 to 45 minutes from my home, depending on the traffic and time of day. For years, I made a point to get there two or three times a week. That worked great when my business was slow, and I had more time to spare. Then something crazy happened! I got what I had been hoping for (more clients) and that kind of time was no longer a luxury I could afford. The solution? Some inexpensive gym flooring, an exercise bike, and a yoga mat in my basement did the trick. Now I have no excuse. At home, I don't get the camaraderie of the studio, to be sure, but I DO have the time to walk downstairs and take care of myself when my workday doesn't permit a trip to the studio or a gym. Most days, that is enough.

E-books and newspapers. Keep reading materials on your phone or in your car for those times when waiting can't be avoided. Rather than perusing old magazines at the doctor's office, why not catch up on professional reading?

How long does that take? Think about the appointments you have set and the people you are meeting. Build in a little cushion between appointments that are likely to run long. If someone you must meet with tends to be late or likes to talk, schedule accordingly—and bring along a book or laptop in case they get stuck in traffic.

Google it! Before spending time and money or trying to do something yourself, be sure to look for instructions, product reviews, etc. on the Internet. My son once told me that today, there is really no excuse for not knowing something. At least the basics on most topics can be found in a five-minute search. You can even do this from your phone while waiting in line at the grocery store.

Automatic coffee. If you have appliances with timers, you can often set your day in motion the night before. When I am really on my game and know I have an early obligation, I like to set up my coffee pot to come on by itself in the morning. Measuring the coffee and filling it takes just a few minutes when I am fully awake, but in the morning while I am still sleepy? Well, let's just say that cleaning up the spills that come from me trying to do anything in the kitchen before I'm really awake takes up extra time.

Reserve early for special occasions. Since most people travel over the holidays, be sure to reserve your accommodations, flights, kennel for the dog, etc. early. Waiting can mean making multiple calls to find what you need, and *who has time for that?*

Automation nation. Some technologies are real game changers in our personal lives. Take, for example, the vacuuming robot. At first glance, it seems frivolous . . . until you realize that for what it costs to hire a housekeeper for two or three visits, you can come home every single day to a house that has just been vacuumed—without having to nag your kids to do it. If your budget allows for it, this invention can return a few needed hours to your week.

Warning: Even a perfectly functional, well-programmed robot can get into trouble. I have a sweet old dog named Spot, and one day I was late getting home to let her out. Have you ever wondered what happens when a vacuuming robot steps in poo? To make a long, messy story short, I will just say that if you have pets, it may make sense to program it to run when you are at home—just in case.

Can the spam! Check the settings on your spam filter in your email program. If you own your domain, see what kind of spam filters you can add to the server as well. Who has time to delete the ads for curing ailments you don't have, anyway?

Train your phone. If you use voice recognition on your phone or computer, taking a few minutes to train the software can save tons of aggravation and little (and big) snippets of time looking up phone numbers or making corrections to dictated documents. It can also save you from swearing at the voice recognition software when it accidentally dials an old boyfriend because it misunderstood you. *Cancel! Cancel! Cancel! That's NOT what I said!*

Prioritize and plan. Don't be too rigid, but at the beginning of each day and at the start of each week, think about how you will use the hours available to you—for work, for play, for activities that blur the lines between the two. Set aside chunks of time to use deliberately, whether that means developing a research proposal, answering email, or binge-watching your favorite TV show.

Sticky notes and mirror-writing. I have been known to put sticky notes in places where I know that I will see them, and to write major goals on my mirror in dry erase marker, where I will be reminded of the day's focus while brushing my teeth. When I went through a period where the allure of streaming season after season of my favorite television shows was a little too tempting for me, I even put a sticky note that read, "NO!" on the screen of my television. It served to remind me not to fall prey to the mind-numbing distraction that I had trouble turning off sometimes. This trick works at the office, at home, or anywhere where you can leave yourself a note without a lot of external judgment.

Pretty keys save time. I know it can seem frivolous or even dumb to consider buying a Darth Vader house key, but consider this question. How many times have you fumbled through the junk drawer wondering where all those keys go, unable to find the spare house key to give the pet sitter as you rush to catch your flight?

What did that cost you in terms of time and aggravation? If you are not inclined to spend a few extra dollars on weird-looking keys, simply mark the important ones with a drop of nail polish to help you remember what they go to.

Schedule magic. If you are in charge of your schedule, or if you can get away from the office at lunch, try to run errands during the day when the lines at the post office, grocery store, etc., are shorter.

Form a healthy relationship with social media. Are you and Facebook seeing too much of each other? If you realized this morning that you lost an hour watching silly videos, you might need to set a timer. Are you on Facebook to promote your business or check out your high school sweetheart? Just sayin' . . . Many of us use social media strategically, to promote business campaigns, support our colleagues' endeavors, and stay abreast of what is happening in our communities, both communities of practice and our home towns. This is not only a positive thing, but necessary for most of us. Yet there is always a danger of getting lost in these interactions, looking up, and noticing that two hours have passed and we still haven't started on a critical project. Social media breaks can be a welcome, even needed, distraction during the day, as long as we are conscious of the time we are spending and how.

Maintain your car. If you own an automobile, make the time for oil changes and routine maintenance. You can work or read in the waiting room, and it is cheaper and less time-consuming than breaking down on the way to work. Tow trucks can take a very long time to arrive, and who has the time to deal with getting a rental or arranging for rides while your car is in the shop, especially if it could have been prevented?

Fix it or get rid of it. For years I set aside broken items, especially things that were expensive when purchased, for the day when I would magically have time to fix them. The result? A big basket of junk and obsolete electronics sitting atop the washer collecting dust and nagging at me each time I did laundry, not to mention an old work printer and computer that are still cluttering up my storage space. (Good grief!) If it doesn't work or is obsolete, ask yourself if you have the time, skills, or inclination to work on it. If the answer is yes, do it on the spot or schedule time to do so within a day or two. If you can't or won't take care of it now, do you really want to have to dust it or carve out time later on to deal with the mess? If you are not willing to deal with it, then maybe it's time to get rid of it.

App-tastic! If you use a smartphone and or smart watch, be "smart" about how you use it! Get rid of the apps you don't use and arrange your displays so that the useful ones are easy to find.

Do not disturb. Carefully consider which notifications you turn on and off to make the most of your technology. If every news app or social media feed is allowed to send you notifications, you may find that you are constantly being interrupted. Ask yourself questions like, "Do I want to be interrupted during my work day when someone posts a new dancing cat video?" or "What about natural disasters or flood warnings close to my location?"

Gym bag, yoga mat, water bottle . . . CHECK! If you are always on the run, why not throw some sneakers in the car, along with whatever you need to squeeze in a little exercise without making the trip back home to get your belongings. If you are near the yoga studio or gym and a client cancels, you are ready to go and squeeze in some precious *me time*.

Clean your house and office. Who has ten minutes to look for the car keys on the way out the door? Trying to keep things neat decreases the lost time tied to the search for lost items. Oh, and if you can't find your glasses, always check your nose first! (Yep! Done that!) Admittedly, I struggle with this one, myself. I have a very clear trend, though. When the house and car get messy, I know I am overextended and need to prioritize the use of my time better.

Unplug. When you have a lot of people contacting you and plenty of work that requires you to focus, try unplugging completely for short periods of time. Even if you are on call for a family member and can't be 100% unreachable, it can be helpful to turn off the Wi-Fi and silence your work phone while you work on a big project, just like you would if you were in an important meeting. In general, you can respond to emails within 24 hours and voicemails the same work day without incident. I even mark out time on my calendar to return calls, so I don't forget.

Ask your kids. As embarrassing as this is, Gen X-ers, when it comes to information technology, ask your teenager for help before you spend four hours trying to do something involving computers or social media. Even for those of us who think of ourselves as tech-savvy, we learned computers as a second language and our kids are digital natives. Not only can you save time and money by tapping into your children's expertise, it does great things for a child's self-esteem to help Mom solve an aggravating problem. Double win!

WHEN BUSINESS BECKONS

For many years, I worked part-time in an organization where part-time work was almost unheard of. To be fair, I had sacrificed half of my salary and benefits to do so. Yet there was a fair amount of resentment from some of my co-workers when they saw me leaving at two in the afternoon to go pick up my kids. My solution? I vowed to be as productive in my 20 hours of flex-time per week, as the typical 40-hour employee. Apart from being exhausting, my strategy worked, and I remained in that job until I quit to focus on my doctoral dissertation several years later. Whether you are a super-charged part-time employee or a full-time staff member trying to squeeze it all in without working an 80-hour week, this section is for you! It is divided into two sections: ideas for saving time at the office and ideas for saving time on the road (for those of us who know our boarding groups without even looking at the plane ticket).

Which of these ideas you can actually implement depends on the kind of job you currently have. For example, when I worked in the aerospace industry, doing work on an airplane was strictly off limits. Now, as a self-employed consultant, I can work anywhere . . . and I do! Remember that this is not a book that is designed to be read from cover to cover, or a series of steps that are guaranteed to work in any situation. Pick the ideas that appeal to you, the ones that seem to fit your particular situation. Try them and see what sticks. If you try something and it doesn't resonate with you, let it go. I won't be offended at all. I'll be thrilled that you found your next steps, the ones that work for you personally! So here goes! Let's try it!

AT THE OFFICE/IN THE SHOP

Smooth out your processes. If you are doing something for the first time, but expect to do it again, keep some notes about what you learned for future reference. If you already have a documented process and timeline for a large task, be sure to refine it over time and capture the learning, so you don't have to reinvent the wheel each and every time—unless you enjoy pain, in which case, "Go for it!"

Do a good job the first time around. Rework is frustrating, time-consuming, and usually does not result in additional revenue. A little attention to detail at the front end of a project can save you a lot of time later on.

Keep good customers. Think about how much time it takes to find a new client. Keeping your existing clients happy is easier and can bring referrals. You might have to get some help with this or use a contact manager, but the follow through is worth it.

Take the time to train your staff properly. If you are in a position where you must count on others to get a job done, a little time spent in training them upfront can help you avoid a host of problems, including rework, poor customer service, safety issues, and more. As a bonus, time and/or money that you invest in training sends a strong message to workers that they are valued and appreciated.

Get therapy for the love–hate relationship between you and your calendar. If you use an electronic calendar, try adding alerts to tell you what time to leave for appointments, reminders the day before to do some preparation, and attachments so that you have the needed references at your fingertips. For some of us, this isn't enough. I am one of those people, so I also have my assistant go over my obligations with me twice a week to prevent double booking.

Be picky about whom you choose to work with. Not everyone can or should collaborate with you. If you accept an arrangement where you do the lion's share of the work, be sure you know exactly what you are getting into and that the payoff is worth it. For a consultant, that means reading reviews of businesses you are considering working for or with and politely declining if there are any significant red flags. It can also mean paying attention to would-be joint venture partners to determine whether they can be trusted to do what they say they will do. It can be hard to say no to someone who wants to hire you or collaborate with you, but walking away months later is more difficult and costs you money (in the form of opportunity costs and cash both) and precious time.

Use a timer. If you are one of those people who works on several projects at once, it can be helpful to use a timer to track project time by client. I use a timer on my phone to track how long I spend on each task. This time-tracking provides valuable information when it comes to planning future efforts. It also helps me assess how well I am managing my time, and to be honest when billing clients by the hour.

Keep up with the books. I struggle with this one myself. The fact is that a few minutes here and there and a little focused time each week can go a long way to limiting the number of queries from your tax accountant and bookkeeper. If you keep your own books, consider it a way to avoid the three-day nightmare of reconciling a big pile of receipts at the end of the year. This is not my forte, and I have to carve out time to deal with my receipts before tax time rolls around—I tend to ignore my own advice in this area. Guilty as charged!

Be concise. We all know the pain of politely listening to someone who is long-winded, even if we love what he or she is talking about. Honor other people's time by thinking about your message and explaining it clearly. This is not easy. It requires work up front, but when it is your turn to speak, try this. See if you can spend less time getting to the point, while still honoring the other person's need to have their responses heard. People will appreciate it! Better yet, many will return the favor.

Outsource the things that bog you down. Entrepreneurs: Can you hire a bookkeeper, find an assistant, or pay an outside service? If so, you can free up valuable hours for more creative work. This one also works if you have a regular J-O-B. Think about outsourcing the shopping by using a mail order service, having someone else clean or run errands for you, or even getting one of those nifty vacuuming robots.

Sync your devices. If you are a tech-dependent worker, like so many of us are these days, be sure to sync important files. Back them up to a cloud-based storage system if your company's security measures don't prevent you from doing so. Why? If you find yourself stranded somewhere with only your smartphone or the computer in a hotel business center, you can get work done more easily and avoid losing time, which would be the case because you don't have what you need. Easy access to critical files equates to less time wasted.

Get the training. How much time do you spend trying to figure things out for yourself? If you are working on your business and consider your time to be valuable, as you should, then maybe it is time to pay a web designer or virtual assistant instead of doing everything yourself. If that isn't in the budget, at least consider spending a little time with the tutorials or take a class or two so that you can learn the shortcuts and workarounds for your software.

Likewise, for those things you absolutely must do yourself, seek out experts to help you become really good at them.

Think strategically about multi-tasking. It can be tempting to multi-task, particularly if you have a military operations background where you may have dealt with multiple inputs at once. Sometimes that works fine, but when you are doing creative work or challenging tasks, it can be a bad idea. Multi-tasking can also make us more prone to accidents; for example, forgetting that dinner is on the stove while answering an email—not that I have ever done that . . . .

De-clutter your electronics! It may not get as dusty, but your electronic desktop can be a mess too. If you routinely spend extra time looking for work files, take a few moments to organize things in folders and tag files with keywords. Change obscure titles to file names that will mean something to you a year from now, when you search for them for use in some new project you haven't even thought of yet. Decide what items need to be accessible from the cloud and use apps to be sure you can get to them from any device.

Front load your work! Got a deadline? Start the work early. That way if the task is more complicated than you thought or if you hit a snag, you are still on time! It is way less stressful to deal with a problem a week before the due date than three hours before your publisher's deadline!

Pause to be kind and friendly. As we work ourselves into a frenzy, trying to do more and more in less and less time, it can be easy to become short-tempered with our coworkers, especially if they interrupt us now and again. Remember that there are different types of personalities in the workplace. Some people get right to the point, while others need to chat for a few minutes before they can get down to business. Dismissing these people can prevent you from getting what you need today and might result in your inability to get their help later on. Yes. It pays to make time to connect with others. Not only will you be more likely to get help and collaborate more effectively, but you might also make your life richer by adding some nice people to your social circles. What if five minutes of listening to someone talk about his kids today saves you three hours tomorrow when he likes you enough to share useful information?

Visit http://www.myersbriggs.org/ to learn more about personality types and how they affect workplace interactions.

Schedule office time. Rather than popping into and out of your email account and paperwork all day long, try scheduling blocks of time to take care of correspondence, bills, bookkeeping chores, etc. As I noted earlier, most people expect an email or telephone response within twenty-four hours and few will be offended by a call back later the same day, especially if that short delay allows you to meet your deadlines.

Back up your files. If you can't afford the time to rewrite it, make a backup copy. Likewise, be sure that if you are faced with a crashed system or stolen laptop, you will be able to restore everything with minimal loss. Whether that means—an online backup, hard drives on the desk, or both—backup often, very often. You don't want to lose a couple of days of productivity when you are facing a client deadline. When working on a large project, I typically save each draft with the date in the subject line so that I can revert to it later on if a revision goes awry. It also provides solace (and salvation) when a large manuscript or another critical file is corrupted in the eleventh hour.

I recall being in the laboratory with some classmates during the final days before our masters' theses were due. A few of us painfully discovered our word-processing program's file size limitations, which turned all of our images into large red *Xs*. There was, admittedly, some foul language involved as we recreated the diagrams and reverted to earlier drafts of our documents. For those who had not saved their files often, the act of recreating the work of the last few, frantic weeks must have been tough.

If it isn't working out for you, consider not doing it! As an entrepreneur, I was very much in love with my first business, what I now consider my "starter business." It took a very long time to get it up and running. There was a whole lot of learning and discovery in the mix, everything from product development to sales, branding, customer relations, etc. As my naiveté wore off, something that took entirely too long, I began to implement the techniques from my business training and days of managing technical efforts in the aerospace industry. The business started to pick up at last! However, it had taken me so long that I had begun to see the company's name as synonymous with *frustration and struggle*. My heart was no longer in it. The only way forward was to close it out and start fresh with an entirely new approach. There are worse things than hanging up an unproductive business entity. Honestly! You get to take the lessons forward with you and start fresh. That's a gift.

Be prepared! My sons were Boy Scouts, and I love this part of that organization's philosophy. Print out extra copies of materials when meeting with colleagues and come prepared with your questions and what you want to accomplish. Doing this simple thing can help to speed things along. In my experience, ten minutes of preparation on my part can cut a two-hour meeting down to 30 minutes, especially if others come prepared as well.

Double-duty. If you are having trouble fitting in time to take care of your health, why not do some of your reading on a stationary bike or elliptical machine? Granted, you won't have the best cardio workout of your life while reading, but you can get through that book your boss suggested and burn a calorie or two.

The joys of clear nail polish and an extra pantyhose. Keep a kit in your car with a few basics. Nail polish will stop tights or nylons from running further if you paint a line around the hole or snag. If you wear a lot of dresses, an extra pair of hose in the glove compartment can be a life-saver when you are in a hurry and have no opportunity to run home and change before that all-important interview or presentation.

Master the basics. Some tasks are basic building blocks for other tasks. Just as when we learn mathematics, where it pays to learn the basics by heart before moving on to more complicated topics like calculus, it can also pay to master the basics in any other field—including business. For instance, if you have your own business, the elevator speech is key. It's a building block consisting of the ability to clearly state your value proposition. If you don't outsource public relations work, consider creating a schedule and repeatable processes so you can be ready with timely press releases, web content, and content marketing that maintain consistency with your brand.

Remember, no effort is wasted. Keep old proposals, course papers, etc. You never know when you can dust them off and use them as the starting point for a new project. (Note: If you publish, be sure to cite yourself to avoid self-plagiarism.)

Know what your time is worth. Know your hourly rate and consider the time spent in ways that don't generate revenue or further your purpose. Think in terms of opportunity cost. "If my time is worth $X per hour, can I afford to use that time doing this task or attending this event?"

The gift of asynchronous communications. If you are in a hurry and have a thirty-second message to pass along, an email or voicemail can often do the trick, particularly if you don't have time for a long conversation. Likewise, sending a card or flowers to a talkative relative allows you to be affectionate and supportive even though you don't necessarily have an hour to spare.

A little follow up can save a lot of time spent correcting misunderstandings. Take the time to communicate clearly, via multiple paths when it's important. When there is a lot to say, and it needs to be explained in writing, it sometimes pays to send it via email, then follow-up by phone. Likewise, after an important face to face or phone meeting, recap the important points via email while they are fresh in your mind. This simple act can help you make sure everyone is on the same page, clarify things if you are not, and—in the event that there are trust issues—document what was agreed to. Misunderstandings and emotional reactions to confusion are huge time-wasters.

ON THE ROAD

Getting there is half the fun! Check travel times for driving, walking, or taking public transportation from one meeting to the next using an online mapping program or app. Add ten minutes to allow for traffic and unexpected delays, more if you are in a large city or are taking a bus. If you arrive early, you can use the time to prepare for the meeting, meditate, or read something of value.

Be deliberate about your travel time. I used to always buy the cheapest airline tickets possible, just thinking about the money. So I would end up taking ridiculous routes across the country, sometimes with tired little kids in tow, losing many productive hours and tanking family morale in the process. You might still end up buying the cheapest tickets, but I would challenge you to consider flight time as part of the equation. For business travel, it can also make sense to buy a First Class seat or trade some precious air miles for an upgrade if you need to work and/or have a critical meeting the same day.

Call your taxi the night before. When traveling, use the hotel's concierge service to help you secure transportation. You can arrange your cab the night before, know that the company hired will be reputable and safe, and not have to get up at four in the morning only to find that there are no cabs available to get you to the airport. Missing a flight is time-consuming.

Make the train car your library. Headphones and a little pre-planning can allow you to find an extra hour or two for research if you are in a place where taking public transportation makes sense. Set the alarm on your watch or phone to avoid missing your stop and pay attention to safety cues. If your *Spidey sense* is going off, maintain situational awareness and do the reading later—but in most cases, trains and busses are great places to digest new material while getting from place to place.

Plan your route for efficiency. If you have a meeting across town, try to pick up dry cleaning or office supplies on the way back or, better yet, book two appointments close to each other to reduce the number of trips back and forth across town.

Memorization nation. If you have a speech to memorize, why not turn it into the equivalent of your favorite song? I make the most of the prep time for high-pressure events by recording my speech and then listening to it while I sleep, reinforced by playing it in the car and while exercising as well. Soon I find myself talking along with it, like singing along with my favorite song. (Safety first, again! Seriously—eyes on the road, you!)

Do I really want to go there? It can be easy to commit to conferences and business trips if you love to travel like I do. They are bright shiny objects to me, opportunities for adventure. As more and more of these things pop up, I find that I have to be more selective. Some trips cost me money. Others make me money. When there are a lot of trips I am tempted to take, it is necessary to think things through. How much do I want to be on the road? If I travel twice in one month, what am I giving up in terms of getting things done back at the office? Can I still accomplish all of that if I am on the road? How much time do I lose to rescheduling routine commitments for each trip?

Use that club pass. Many of us have benefits from our credit cards that we forget to use. I used to let those airline frequent flier club cards go unused on occasion, always saving them for that horrible layover I would have to cope with on some later trip that I hadn't yet booked. These days, if I have an hour to kill, I will use the passes. I get some work done and even get a meal without spending a fortune on junk food I didn't really want. Time saved? Five to ten minutes in line at an airport restaurant, plus a few minutes of extra productivity as I work in a less crowded, more pleasant environment than the seating area at the gate. Sometimes I even get to meet interesting people while I wait.

Car cleaning. I used to know a woman who spent many hours each day in gridlock on the highway. She kept some window cleaner and dusting supplies in the car for those occasions. Why not make the most of the time if you find yourself sitting still for an hour waiting for traffic to clear? (Note: I am not advocating window-cleaning while in motion! Be safe out there.)

Timeshare? Work there! Many people have a hard time carving out time for their most important tasks. Creative projects like books, dissertations, and academic writing require chunks of time in relative isolation for most of us. If you have access to a timeshare or a relative's cabin or condo, why not book yourself a work-cation? I do this every fall with a couple of trusted colleagues. We work on our individual projects side by side, conveniently out of reach of our day-to-day jobs and interruptions.

Listen up! If you have a road trip coming up, or if you're like me and spend a lot of time driving around town, you can be learning at the same time. Podcasts and audiobooks make great travel companions. You can even listen to the same section more than once if the narrator says something important. (Of course, be sure to pull over before changing the CD or advancing the podcast. Safety first!)

Make reservations. If you are on a tight schedule or meeting with a client at a nice restaurant, be sure to reserve your table in advance to avoid wasting time waiting. You can even reserve tables in many restaurants online before you leave your office or do it in the cab from your phone. Better yet, ask your assistant to set up the logistics for very important client meetings, so you can devote your attention to more important things.

Up in the air? I am one of those people who can always sleep on the airplane. If you have shared a row in economy seating with me, I wholeheartedly apologize for any snoring and drooling that may have occurred during our flight. Each time we get on a plane, we have choices. Is it nap time? Is it reading time? Writing time?

Chat time with the interesting person (potential friend or even client) in the seat next to me? Airplane time need not be wasted time, whether we use it to recharge our batteries by watching a movie or edit that paper we meant to finish last week.

A Dozen Little Tricks for Caregivers of All Kinds

If you have ever had, or are currently experiencing, the painful honor of holding someone's hand during a difficult time, this section is for you. I call it a painful honor because there is no denying the emotionally draining and time-consuming aspects of upending one's life to take care of a loved one. At the same time, I came to realize, sometime after my parents' deaths, that being a person they were willing and able to turn to when their lives became difficult was one of the greatest gifts a daughter could ever have. The depth of trust and love in my parents' allowing me to help them when they were no longer strong, and even quite afraid, is something I now recall with gratitude. I am glad I could be there for them when they needed me, something I consider to be the true essence of family.

To witness another's pain and offer comfort is no easy task. It strips away our prior notions of what is important and upends reality as we knew it before. My heart goes out to the caretakers among us. Moving forward with kindness and grace while doing something so difficult takes a special kind of person. Not only are such circumstances emotionally difficult, but they also come with new and profound time management challenges. The doctors' appointments, trips to the emergency room, pharmacy runs, and (far more important) long talks that simply cannot wait.

Some of these tips may seem trivial, while others are more profound. If I can save you five minutes here and there, my work is done here! You see, when we are helping someone through the final stages of their journey or raising children, minutes *do* count.

When children are small, it may seem like they will be around for a long time. Having them grown up and gone seems unimaginably far away. Yet here I sit, alone in the house that once was home to two sweet little boys who had the audacity to grow into productive citizens with lives of their own! Seriously, I am happy for them. I am glad they don't need much attention from their mother because when they call, I know it is because they really *do* miss me. My point is that the time when our children are home is every bit as precious as the final stages of life—even more so since childhood sets the stage for a productive life.

Whether you are tending to children, the elderly, or someone with a disability, the caretaker's journey is a stressful one, albeit a meaningful one. Here are a few little ideas to help you fit a little more life into your days while helping others who depend on you.

Extra copies of lists. If your loved one is taking a complex cocktail of prescribed medications or needs to do specific exercises at certain times, a list is often necessary. As we juggle more and more responsibilities, get less and less sleep, and deal with crisis after crisis, it's hard to remember everything. Why not keep extra copies of medication lists in the car, with medical records, and on your phone? I took a photograph of my dad's medication list after each doctor's appointment to capture the most recent changes and kept it on my phone, where it would be handy for filling out the next set of paperwork.

Doctor's office time warps. During my parents' twilight years, I would not enter a building with the word "medical" anywhere in its name or description without bringing along enough work to occupy me for several hours. Depending on the physician or service provider, you really can't count on your appointment time being kept. Often, medical providers are called away for emergencies, leaving their scheduled appointments waiting for anywhere from five minutes or two hours—with no way to predict how long it will take for our loved ones to be seen. I quickly learned not to schedule anything important for at least a few hours past my loved ones' appointment times. If you are accompanying a child, it is always a good idea to have extra toys as well. Of course, when your appointment goes as scheduled, you get time back into your day. Win!

The early bird catches the calendar. If you can get to the doctor's office early in the day, it can be a real time-saver. Think of it this way. If the first few patients of the day are late or have complex problems that take extra time to diagnose, those effects can cascade throughout the day, causing patients with appointments in the afternoon to wait longer and longer to be seen. There have been man occasions where I arrived on time for a two o'clock appointment with my kids and waited until three thirty for the doctor to come rushing in. He was great with patients and worth it in the long run, but the added requirement of entertaining the kids in the waiting room and losing an afternoon's productivity was stressful. Eventually, I cracked the code and started booking the earliest appointments possible. I am not a morning person, but if a doctor or dentist visit is on the agenda, it's worth it to me to be one of the first patients of the day!

Lipstick in your purse. When we are pulled in several directions at once, it can be easy to let ourselves go. I don't have scientific evidence to support this, but I know that when I was going through my "sandwich generation" phase, taking care of parents and kids— and rarely myself—something as simple as a putting on a little lipstick using the car mirror put a spring in my step and made me move just a little bit faster from one task to the next.

Give your kids their own "work to do." When I was working on my master's degree, I remember doing calculus while very pregnant with a three-year-old on my knee. (Oddly enough, the three-year-old grew up to pursue a career in math, something I wasn't very good at myself.) He would watch me for a while and then climb down to go get crayons and "work" on his own papers. It makes sense to pass along extra marketing materials, worksheets, etc. to occupy our kids if we need to work from home. They play at "work," imagining themselves as grownups anyway. So this is a constructive way to channel their energy and still accomplish what you need to as a parent/student/worker/superwoman.

Family phone tree. When my mom was ill, my father gave me a list of people to call in each emergency, and a list of people to ask them to call on my behalf. When a loved one is in the emergency room, worried relatives often want to know what is going on, but if you are the primary caretaker, your attention is needed elsewhere.

If you are also taking care of children and holding down a job, three hours on the telephone in the midst of a crisis won't help you to get it all done. Having a phone tree can help, particularly if your loved one is struggling with a terminal disease where hospital stays are frequent.

Just get the ramp! When my mom was in a wheelchair, a well-meaning family member put together two temporary skids so that I could roll my mother's wheelchair up the front steps of my house. While it did get the job done, the extra time lost struggling with a make-shift solution, then afterward letting go of the frustration of not having what I needed, cost me time that I simply could not afford as a working mother and daughter. Eventually, we replaced the skids with an actual ramp, cutting the time to push her up the front steps dramatically and saving the time I had previously spent complaining.

Coping and processing the journey. When you are in the thick of caring for a loved one who is struggling or busily raising children (or both at once), it can be easy to surround yourself with (and unwittingly create) drama. Drama steals your attention away from getting things done. Trust me! I know what I am talking about here and I have the scars to prove it. If you are coping with grief, family problems, or another kind of trauma, an hour to safely vent with a therapist can help you get back on track to being effective and efficient the rest of the time. Think of it as opening the valve of a pressure cooker *before* the lid goes flying across the room and does some real damage. Dealing with problems in a safe space ultimately saves time because it helps us to avoid time-consuming, unhealthy—even traumatic—interactions with others.

Have it delivered! If you need a particular kind of pen refills, medication, face cream, etc. for those you take care of, don't waste hours combing several stores looking for a hard-to-find item. The cost of delivery is typically less than the value of the hours spent searching for it in person. Just order it online and retrieve it from your front porch. Schedule routine deliveries if your need is predictable so that you only have to deal with it once. Something that I had a difficult time understanding when my parents were ill was how vital it was for them to know what products they were getting. Substituting a brand of over-the-counter medication they know with one they have not come to trust, or worse, risking an allergic reaction to an unexpected product, can be avoided by ordering products ahead of time. When our bodies are struggling just to maintain basic bodily functions, something as simple as the wrong brand of lotion can create another time-consuming trip to the doctor for all concerned, not to mention avoidable pain and stress.

Use your work to recharge your batteries. When my father was undergoing chemotherapy, I was a full-time doctoral student and a mother of two teens, but I made a commitment to support my dad. That meant many long hours by his side at the hospital, surrounded by people who were having a very hard time. By sheer accident, I ended up using the work that I had to do anyway as a source of rejuvenation. I discovered that I could be by my dad's side when he was awake and wanted to talk, but when he fell asleep, I could pull my books and laptop out of my purse and take refuge in my work. Doing so made me productive. It allowed me to be close at hand when he needed me. Most of all, it kept me from dwelling on the difficulty of the situation so that when he awoke, I was feeling good and ready with a much-needed smile and a hug. The sense that I had accomplished a lot during his nap decreased my stress and gave my father a more cheerful companion for the ride home.

Freeze frame! If healthy meals are important to you, and they should be, why not put that freezer compartment to good use? If you are making one pan of lasagna, why not make three? It's a simple matter of economies of scale (nerd alert)! You maximize your payoff for the time spent cleaning the kitchen! There's nothing like coming home from work exhausted, wondering what to feed the kids and then realizing that the work is already done. You pull something delicious out of the freezer, pop it in the oven and knock out a little more work while it cooks, and everybody is happy. One of my best friends is the master of this technique. She will cook, slice, and freeze a week's worth of chicken to add to salads, soups, etc. throughout the week. I used to do it too when my house was full, and I often took meals down the block to my parents' house. Once in a while, I would devote an entire day to making casseroles and soups to lighten my load in the coming days. The payoff in terms of time management without compromising on nutrition was huge!

Close the lid. I used to try and respond to my children while doing my homework. They would get mad, and rightly so. The fact is that once your concentration is broken, you are no longer productive in either situation, with the work or the kids. I finally learned that it is almost always a mistake to continue typing while someone is talking to you. Accept the interruption. Your concentration is broken anyway, and you don't know whether your child is telling you something urgent, *like that the dinner you left on the stove is burning and they want to know where the fire extinguisher is*, or something else. In the eyes of a child, it's all pretty important, and they need your support. Finally, after my sons complained enough, I developed the habit of closing my laptop after verbalizing something like, "Let me save this quickly and close down the machine so I can focus on what you are saying." This response works with coworkers too. The work is saved. The person who has walked in feels respected, and your eyes are on them, not the machine or the message to someone who is not actually present in the room with you at that moment. How does that save time? It

helps you avoid arguments, hurt feelings, and the need to apologize,

both in the moment and over the long-haul.

FOR THE NON-TRADITIONAL STUDENT

I remember hearing my teenagers complain about their assignments one night and then smugly saying, "Wanna trade?"

Going back to school with kids in the house is tough, rewarding, and inspirational. When we choose the path of life-long learning, we redefine the boundaries of age and expectation for everyone we know. Our children learn to set their sights higher as they see our example. Friends witness our growth and branch out in other ways, some growing closer to us and others wishing us a fond farewell, whether permanently or temporarily. We forge new relationships with colleagues who inspire us as they too strive for more and more over time. Whether you go back for a new degree every decade (my pattern), started college late in life, or simply decided to go to school in your thirties, I salute you. We are the late bloomers who surprise others by blooming in our OWN season! That comes with its own gifts (e.g., being a bona fide grown up with focus and dedication when you hit the books), and some time-management challenges we might not have had straight out of high school. Here are a few ideas I picked up while walking that path. Enjoy!

First things first. Personal drama and health problems are a common cause for not finishing a degree program. In many cases, these can be avoided by planning ahead and communicating with loved ones. Before taking on a major, long-term obligation, it can be useful to contract with your family about the time that will be needed to study, the time they need from you, and the time you will need to keep your body healthy. Doing this won't lengthen the day beyond 24 hours, sadly, but it will help you to avoid losing the people and things that matter most along the journey. Again, drama, sickness, and ultimately remorse, are all very time-consuming.

Frontload your work. When I give advice to adult students, I often tell them to frontload their work. When you get the syllabus, dive in. Try to read the books before the quarter begins. Why? As more seasoned students, our challenges are different than they were in our teens and twenties. If we frontload our work and then, as the due date approaches, we have one of those nights where the dog throws up on the carpet, our spouse is out of sorts, the kids need help with homework . . . (You get the gist.), we still have something to turn in and can pass our classes. Conversely, if we wait until the last minute to start a big assignment and life gets in the way, then we are at the mercy of the professor, who may or may not sympathize with our plight.

The notepad in your purse. Whether you prefer a traditional pen and paper or the voice recorder on your phone, it can be good to have a way to record random but potentially useful thoughts that come up at inconvenient times. The big idea you needed for your class paper or your dissertation may come while you are at a red light or in the middle of a three-mile jog. Having a way to pull over and record the flash of brilliance before it can escape is a life-saver!

Check yourself. As a teacher, I can tell you that plagiarism is a very big deal. Among adult students who have been out of the classroom for a while, the rules are sometimes unclear. It pays to ask questions in this area because accidentally submitting work that looks suspiciously like something that's available on the internet or a paper that was turned in at another university has ended many, many academic careers. We read so much that it can be difficult to remember what we learned about from whom. The solution? First, if you are writing a lot, it can be good to keep an annotated bibliography. An annotated bibliography is a document (or database) that includes the citations of all of the books and articles you have read, what the key concepts were, and what you thought about them. (I use Thompson Reuters' Endnote.) Second, if your university offers a plagiarism checker, use it—for every single paper! Librarians usually have access to a service like Turnitin.com, even if you don't. I was also pleased to learn that Grammerly.com not only checks grammar now, but the paid version also has a plagiarism checker. It's worth every penny to avoid the time lost trying to explain yourself to your professor or the dean in case of an accidental match. These programs allow you to quickly find these types of errors first and revise your wording before you turn in your paper.

Find like-minded study buddies. When you are doing something very taxing, like working on an advanced degree, it can be helpful to team up with workmates who are on similar paths. I have spent many hours in the company of like-minded friends working side by side with headphones on in coffee shops, ski lodges, and living rooms. The presence of a colleague can be a real productivity boost if you are both sufficiently focused to stay on task. You have someone to give a quick opinion if needed. You can check one another's progress and motivate each other to get things done. For example, one of my colleagues was working with me in this fashion recently, and she knew that I had spent a few hours longer than I meant to on a particular task. At one point in the day, she checked in with me to see if I had moved on yet. I had, thankfully, but if I hadn't, her gentle question would have gotten me back on track.

Outsourcing at home. If you are taking care of multiple people, whether that means children, grandparents, or someone else, you probably need some help—especially if you are juggling all of that along with a job and/or school. During some of the busiest times of my life, when I had the resources to do so, I took the plunge to hire a housecleaning service. Of course, you have to be picky, using referrals and finding someone who is bonded and insured, but the relief of coming home from work to a clean-smelling house can be huge. A friend with small children put it this way, "I like to know that no matter what kind of a week I am having, the toilets will at least be clean."

Don't read academic papers like you would read novels. I really struggle with this one. My learning preferences border between global and sequential. That means that I love the big picture, but when I read, I have a tendency to go line by line, from start to finish. This method takes way too much time and isn't the most efficient way to process the salient points of a scholarly article. There are a lot of methods out there, and it's worth looking into the different ways to read scholarly work early on. Look for a method that draws your attention to the parts of the article that mean the most to you in your research, whether that means you focus more on the methodology or the results. Ask yourself up front, why am I reading this article? What do I hope to accomplish?

Leverage your personal learning preferences. There are a lot of different learning assessments available on the Internet, and it can be very helpful to examine what methods of learning work best for you. (I was exposed to Neuidentity's Brain Pathways years ago and found it very useful.) As an adult learner, you have to make the most of the study time you have. Taking a simple assessment can help you to figure out what works best for you personally. For some people, it is important to see the material in writing or pictures, perhaps drawing mind maps. Other people need to engage physically or hear the information spoken. Understanding your personal preferences is not a path toward eliminating other ways of learning, especially within the constraints of an accredited program. It shouldn't limit you in any way. Instead, it can tell you how to reinforce the material you are exposed to and engage with it so that you remember things better, maximizing the impact of your study time.

Outline first. If you find yourself doing a lot of writing, it can be helpful to outline your papers/books first, then fill in information in the right place in the document as it comes to you. The right information doesn't always present itself to you in an order that allows you to write an entire paper or book sequentially. Having the literary equivalent of buckets to put the information in as you find it saves a lot of time for the prolific writer. That doesn't mean you won't have to rearrange things as you edit, but it may save you a few iterations on the way to a well-organized paper. (Be sure to cite your sources if you are using ideas that came from other places—again, doing it as you go along can be much faster than trying to find a book or paper from the stack on your desk a month later when asked to cite it.)

LONG-TERM LIFE HACKS

S ome the most impactful time-savers are really about solving more deeply rooted problems. What does *that* mean? I'm glad you asked! These are the problems that show up over and over if we don't pay attention. We sometimes continue to repeat the same mistakes over many years, losing a great deal of time cleaning up the same messes over and over again. Often these problems are rooted in deeply held beliefs that can be traced to an early experience or some aspect of our culture. This belief encourages us to unwittingly repeat an old pattern of behavior even as we change our circumstances. It comes out in big and small ways. Sometimes, it is so insignificant as to escape our notice. Other times, it is writ large for the whole world to see. Just like anything else in nature, people tend to repeat patterns of behavior in big and small ways over time. (For more information, watch my TEDx talk, The Fractal Challenge, at

https://www.youtube.com/watch?v=3F48rvdQMQA)

If we just deal with the problems on the surface, merely treating the symptoms, we may unwittingly cause ourselves to experience these same problems over and over again until we get serious about figuring out why. My doctoral work was all about looking for the kinds of behaviors and perceptions that repeat in big and small ways in organizations and professional networks. With that in mind, I consider this to be the most important part of the book! Here are some long-term time hacks, some of which amount to life hacks, ones that yield lasting benefits.

Get to the heart of repeating issues. Sometimes when we keep slaying the same dragon day after day, there is an underlying issue that is contributing to the repeated headaches. Maybe you need to make the time to train your staff better or document recurring tasks in your business. If you keep losing time to the same issue, think about that. Ask, "What's going on underneath the surface that breathes life into this nagging, time-wasting problem?" Then focus your attention there.

Think of your time in terms of opportunity cost. If I have a dollar in my pocket and put it into a vending machine for some junk food, the opportunity cost of that purchase is everything else I could have done with that dollar. I could have donated it to charity, given it to my son, put it in the bank, or bought an apple at the grocery store instead. I made a choice, and now that dollar is gone. Maybe I am happy with my choice. I was famished, and now I am not. Maybe I made a mistake and soon realize that I needed that dollar to feed the parking meter and avoid a ticket.

Think of your time this way as well. If I am working on this book, I am not moving toward completion on other products, some of which have deadlines and client expectations tied to them. Likewise, if I take on a new client, I am choosing to do that instead of writing another book during those hours. The list goes on! When we think about our time this way, we are conscious not only of what we are choosing to do, but also the things we could have done instead. That can lead to different choices. We turn off the autopilot and think about where each effort is taking us, then budget our time accordingly.

Just say NO! How much time do we lose to things we truly don't want to do? Not only do those tasks take time away from what matters, but the dread and procrastination also interfere with our productivity on a much deeper level. Finding the courage to say, "No, but thank you for the opportunity," is an area I also am working on. It's the secret to avoiding feelings of guilt and overwhelm, and ultimately preserving your integrity.

Don't hold a grudge. Being angry, even if it is justified, wastes a lot of time. Don't be a pushover, but remember not to let people who annoy you rent valuable space in your head. When you need to be working or sleeping, try not to obsess over a slight or personality clash. Instead, communicate your concerns respectfully and assertively when appropriate and then *let it go*. You may have to make a note to revisit an issue if it is necessary to the task at hand, but you are unlikely to get your boss to quit being a jerk by telling him off in your mind at three in the morning instead of getting your beauty sleep.

Take a course online. If going back to school is in the cards, and you need to keep your day job, why not try an asynchronous form of learning? Online programs offer discussion boards that allow you to catch up and join the class discussion at three in the morning without waking up the professor. The long-term implications are that you become a life-long learner, continuously building your skills and becoming more valuable to your employer and collaborators alike. It's also fun!

Laugh more. Have you ever noticed how much longer things take and how much harder they are when you take yourself too seriously? Lighten up, and people will be more inclined to listen to what you have to say. That cuts down on time you have to spend convincing others and can lead to many wonderful surprises. If sales are necessary for your line of work, I can't overstate the time-saving impact of this idea. The more you make people feel good and lighthearted in your presentations the fewer presentations you will have to do.

Network strategically. Choose the social groups and events you attend strategically. Will your clients (current and future) actually be there? How can you be of service to these people and what will you gain? There may be some groups you try to attend every week, while some others may merit popping in once a quarter or sending someone else from your organization to attend. Other groups you will attend just for social reasons—because you really, truly like the people. Either way, don't waste your time in groups where you don't enjoy being there; people can spot a phony a mile away!

Find a mentor ... or three or four. I recently learned how many successful business people have multiple coaches and mentors. It is not unusual to have an academic mentor, a career coach, a PR mentor, sales coaches, an accountability partner, several peer-mentors (trusted friends and colleagues), and a few admired business people who are there for you when I need them. So many of my own failures—let's rephrase that as *learning opportunities—*

could have been prevented had I thought to ask for advice up front. Stay close with those wise and caring people who want to see you succeed, and for Pete's sake, *ask them questions*! Not doing so has cost me months of my time and an embarrassing chunk of my savings account.

Create space for serendipity. Are you truly open to the opportunity of a lifetime when it shows up? Are you too busy to answer the door when opportunity knocks? Do you even hear it? If you are like me, there have been multiple missed opportunities tied to not feeling ready just yet. So leave a little space. Create a little slack in the rope for that ideal opportunity when it surprises you, as good fortune is bound to do.

You catch more flies with honey than vinegar! Credit for this one goes to my mom. As a child, I was always reminded of the need to be kind, even when I was out of sorts. The fact is that things take longer when you need help and you haven't always been helpful to other people. Besides, apologies take a long time. Every step of making amends takes time: all of that worrying, crafting the message, then talking to the offended party, and agonizing over the outcome if it doesn't go well. This is valuable time that could have spent happily working, maybe even alongside the offended party. Who has the time to be nasty to people?

Plan time for family and friends. People you love will appreciate this one. Schedule them in. Planning a regular date night or kid time will reduce the likelihood of an excessive number of emergency calls and interruptions tied to family problems. Maintaining your relationships honors their importance and also helps you to make sound decisions about managing your own time.

Understand the difference between long-term ties (personal and professional) and transactional relationships. This one is BIG. Many people we do business with are nice enough and can provide us with an immediate benefit. There is nothing wrong with interactions that serve the purpose of fostering business transactions only—as long as everyone involved understands that's what going on. Spending too much time with people whose intent is to upsell you can put you at risk, especially if you are in a vulnerable situation personally. If you are going through a difficult time in your life, keep your guard up and make sure you are confiding in friends— not simply service-providers who ask personal questions. The time and productivity wasted on feelings of betrayal or being used are luxuries that none of us can afford.

Self-love. This is not an ego thing at all. The fact is that self-criticism takes up a lot of time and robs us of energy. You don't have to be Brigitte Bordeaux or Kino to be beautiful and fit or Albert Einstein to be smart. Simply appreciate what you bring to the table and work to make the most of your talents—easier said than done. I get that! No more beating yourself up when it's time to get a good night's sleep! *Capiche?*

Exercise and eat right. Can you afford a week in the hospital? If an unplanned week off would wreak havoc on your work, then plan small chunks of time on a daily basis to take care of your body. Allow yourself sufficient time to sleep. You can sometimes prevent the kinds of health problems that might derail you by forging healthy habits.

COMMENCEMENT

C ongratulations! If you are still reading, you have apparently made a commitment to improving your own time management skills. If you skipped around in the book and are quickly perusing the ending to see what is there, that's even better! Why? It means that you are using this resource, and hopefully others like it, strategically, in the way that best serves you. Way to take charge!

Either way, you are taking steps to fit more life into the time you have and moving from being an IBW to becoming an HBW (happily busy woman). How will you know when you get there? Consider taking this little quiz.

APPENDIX: THE INSANELY BUSY WOMAN QUIZ

Give yourself a score between one and five for each of the items below. Then add your scores to see where you fit on the spectrum using the scoring chart below. Are you an *Insanely Busy Woman (IBW), a Happily Busy Woman (HBW),* or somewhere in between?

Questions					Your score
1. You shave off a minute here and an hour there, by putting more efficient and effective processes in place.					
1	2	3	4	5	
Never	Rarely	Sometimes	Most of the time	Always	
2. You know that you can't accomplish everything you want to all at once, but you have learned to prioritize and create the space for what matters most.					
1	2	3	4	5	
Never	Rarely	Sometimes	Most of the time	Always	

3. You don't say yes to every opportunity that presents itself. Instead, you look over your current commitments and consider how much time something will take and whether or not it fits with your overall plan for your life and career.

1	2	3	4	5	
Never	Rarely	Sometimes	Most of the time	Always	

4. You are able to say yes to social engagements with people you genuinely like, and you get there on time too!

1	2	3	4	5	
Never	Rarely	Sometimes	Most of the time	Always	

5. You rarely use the word "should," either taking action to get things done or admitting that a particular task is not at the top of your list.

1	2	3	4	5	
Never	Rarely	Sometimes	Most of the time	Always	

6. You avoid senseless drama and other time-wasters, freeing up your precious moments for the better things in life.

1	2	3	4	5	
Never	Rarely	Sometimes	Most of the time	Always	
				Total :	

Scoring	
6–12 (IBW)	You are a true IBW. It's time to get serious about managing your time and commitments. Begin to look for tasks with finite completion dates. Knock them out and reclaim that time to create some space in your life but saying no to the next project if it isn't something you really, truly want for yourself.
13–18 (HBW Apprentice)	You're still an IBW, but you have come to realize that the light at the end of the tunnel may not be an oncoming train after all. Try some of the simpler time hacks and then build upon these successes to achieve greater mastery.
19–24 (HBW Practitioner)	You're on your way! Perhaps you were an IBW in the past, maybe even the recent past, but you have gained enough awareness to put you on a healthy road to managing your time well. The more progress you make in this area, the more time there is for serendipity. You are beginning to feel calm and happy on a regular basis. There are times when you feel like a Happily Busy Woman, but that's not all of the time.
25–30 (HBW Diva)	You are a true-blue, in-the-flesh HBW. I salute you and look forward to reading YOUR book on the subject. You manage your time very well, achieve much, and prioritize in ways that allow you to manage your emotional energy, not just your calendar!

Now that you are on your way to a happier and more productive life, without tossing aside all of your responsibilities or abandoning your loved ones, it's time to share. Visit me at http://www.tonya.today/ for more insights, tips, and tricks to help you on your journey and join the conversation. I hope that you have enjoyed this book and will use it to your benefit. I firmly believe that by managing the demands on our time better, each of us can improve what we bring to the world as individuals and when we do that from a place of integrity and kindness, everybody wins!